Profiles of the Presidents

JOHN QUINCY ADAMS

★ ★ ★

Profiles of the Presidents

JOHN QUINCY ADAMS

by Michael Burgan

Content Adviser: Caroline Keinath, Deputy Superintendent and Chief of Interpretation, Adams National Historic Site, Quincy, Massachusetts

Reading Adviser: Dr. Linda D. Labbo, Department of Reading Education, College of Education, The University of Georgia

COMPASS POINT BOOKS ✦ MINNEAPOLIS, MINNESOTA

Compass Point Books
3109 West 50th Street, #115
Minneapolis, MN 55410

Visit Compass Point Books on the Internet at *www.compasspointbooks.com*
or e-mail your request to *custserv@compasspointbooks.com*

Photographs ©: White House Collection, Courtesy White House Historical Association, cover, 1; Bettmann/Corbis, 6, 9, 10 (top), 16, 22, 23, 26 (top), 30, 34, 38 (top), 41, 49; Courtesy of the Massachusetts Historical Society, 7 (top); Ann Ronan Picture Library, 7 (bottom), 11, 40; Hulton/Archive by Getty Images, 8, 12, 18, 27, 29, 37, 44, 54 (right), 55, 56 (all), 58; U.S. Department of Interior, National Park Service, Adams National Historical Park, 10 (bottom), 14, 19, 36, 54 (left); Topham Picturepoint, 13; AKG Berlin, 15, 38 (bottom); Images of American Political History, 17, 26 (bottom), 57 (left); Burstein Collection/Corbis, 21; North Wind Picture Archives, 24; Library of Congress, 25, 46, 59 (left); Michael Maslan Historic Photographs/Corbis, 28; Courtesy U.S. Department of the Treasury, 32; Corbis, 33, 42, 45; Stock Montage, 43; Joseph Sohm/Visions of America/Corbis, 47; N. Carter/North Wind Picture Archives, 50; Department of Rare Books and Special Collections, University of Rochester Library, 57 (right); Bruce Burkhardt/Corbis, 59 (right).

Editors: E. Russell Primm, Emily J. Dolbear, Melissa McDaniel, and Catherine Neitge
Photo Researchers: Svetlana Zhurkina and Image Select International
Photo Selector: Linda S. Koutris
Designer: The Design Lab
Cartographer: XNR Productions, Inc.

Library of Congress Cataloging-in-Publication Data
Burgan, Michael.
  John Quincy Adams / by Michael Burgan.
    p. cm.— (Profiles of the presidents)
Summary: A biography of the sixth president of the United States, John Quincy Adams, focusing on his lifetime of public service, including his years in the Senate and House of Representatives and his time in foreign service. Includes bibliographical references and index.
  ISBN 0-7565-0254-3
  1. Adams, John Quincy, 1767–1845—Juvenile literature. 2. Presidents—United States—Biography—Juvenile literature. [1. Adams, John Quincy, 1767–1845. 2. Presidents.] I. Title. II. Series.
  E377 .B87 2003
  973.5'5'092—dc21   2002010000

Table of Contents

★ ★ ★

★

*NOTE: In this book, words that are defined in the glossary are in **bold** the first time they appear in the text.*

A Lifetime of Service

* * *

John Quincy Adams devoted his life to public service. He was the sixth president of the United States. His greatest work, however, came before and after he lived in the White House.

His father was John Adams, the second president of the United States. The younger Adams grew up during the Revolutionary War (1775–1783). He spent his teenage years with his father in Europe and learned several languages. This background helped him when he served as **secretary of**

John Quincy Adams was the sixth president of the United States.

state under President James Monroe. In that job, Adams managed the country's relations with other countries. He also helped expand the borders of the United States.

After serving as president, Adams was elected to the House of Representatives. In the House, he was a strong opponent of slavery. "Slavery," Adams wrote in his diary, "is the great and foul stain upon the North American Union."

The Adams diary is one of the most famous in U.S. history. He started it when he was eleven and kept writing

▲ A page from Adams's diary

◄ Adams was against slavery.

for most of his life. In the diary, Adams recorded his thoughts about the places he visited and the famous people he met. Adams also wrote down his feelings.

To others, Adams seemed stiff and hard to know. His son Charles Francis Adams said his father seemed to wear an "iron mask" that hid his feelings. His diary shows a man who had strong emotions on the inside.

More than anything, Adams wanted to succeed and serve his country the best way he could. "I have always lived with . . . a suitable sense of my duties in society," Adams wrote, "and with a sincere desire to perform them."

Charles Francis ▼
Adams

The President's Son

★ ★ ★

John Quincy Adams was born on July 11, 1767, in Braintree, Massachusetts. (The town is now called Quincy.) He was the second of John and Abigail Adams's five children. By the time John Quincy was born, John Adams was already a well-known Boston lawyer. As a boy, the younger John began signing his name "JADM" so people could tell him apart from his father.

▼ John Quincy's father, John

Both of John Quincy's parents were intelligent. They passed on their love for learning and books to their son. John Adams was

Abigail ▸ Adams

John Quincy ▸ Adams at age fourteen

often away when John Quincy was young, so he and his mother developed a close relationship.

Abigail Adams was a rare woman for her time—she spoke her mind freely on the important political issues of the day. Her son seemed to have picked up his mother's independent spirit. He also shared her Christian beliefs about helping people and doing what was right, no matter what others wanted.

John Quincy Adams grew up seeing British soldiers marching through the streets. When he was young, the United States did not yet exist.

Massachusetts was one of Great Britain's American
colonies. Some people in the colonies were protesting
British laws that they thought were unfair. Protests in
Boston had turned violent, so Great Britain sent troops to
restore order.

◄ *In an event that later became known as the Boston Tea Party, colonists dumped crates of tea into Boston Harbor in 1773 to protest British taxes.*

This led to the American Revolution, which began just outside Boston in April 1775. The Second Continental Congress was called to organize an army to fight the British. John Adams attended the Congress in Philadelphia, Pennsylvania. In July 1776, Adams and the others at the Congress declared the colonies independent from Great Britain. The leaders formed a new country—the United States.

While his father was away, John Quincy became the "man" of the house. He often rode a horse several miles between Braintree and Boston, carrying the family mail. He also felt he had to protect his mother from any British attack.

A detail from John Trumbull's famous painting of the signing of the Declaration of Independence

From a hill near the family farm, John Quincy watched the Battle of Bunker Hill. It was one of the early clashes of the Revolution. Not quite eight years old at the time, John Quincy remembered the scene the rest of his life. Years later he wrote, "I saw with my own

▼ *The Battle of Bunker Hill*

John Quincy Adams ▲
during his trip to
France

eyes those fires . . . and witnessed the tears of my mother."

Late in 1777, Congress decided to send John Adams to France to try to win French support for the Revolutionary War. Adams took John Quincy with him. The trip was dangerous. British warships were patrolling the Atlantic Ocean, looking for U.S. ships. The Adamses' ship avoided the British, but it could not escape stormy seas. John Quincy impressed his father with his bravery during the trip.

John Adams stayed in France a little more than a year. During that time, John Quincy quickly learned French. His father wrote that the boy "learned more French in a day than I could learn in a week with all my books." The boy also studied Latin, **fencing**, dancing, and drawing.

After a brief trip home, the Adamses returned to France. This time at school, John Quincy focused on Greek, Latin, geography, and math. Later, he continued his education in the Netherlands. Then, in 1781, John Quincy was asked to serve as a **translator** for Francis Dana, a U.S. **diplomat** going to Russia. During the late 1700s, the Russian leader, Catherine the Great, spoke French at her court.

▲ *Catherine the Great*

Dana did not speak French well, but John Quincy did. Just fourteen years old, Adams was already able to serve his country.

Adams spent about a year in Russia before returning to the Netherlands in 1783. By then, the American Revolution was over, and his father was finishing work on the peace treaty that would officially end the war. John Quincy studied in Europe another two years before returning to the United States.

At eighteen years old, young John Quincy Adams had seen far more of the world than most older Americans. He was comfortable talking to kings and scholars. His intelligence and charm impressed the people he met. Now, Adams wrote in his diary, he had to think about how "to get my own living in an honorable manner."

First, he attended Harvard College in Cambridge, Massachusetts. He completed his studies there in less than two years. After graduating in 1787, Adams studied to

Adams attended ◄
Harvard College.

become a lawyer, like his father. He passed the law exam in 1790 and began working in Boston.

By then, Adams's father was serving as vice president of the United States under President George Washington. The younger Adams some-times wrote newspaper articles defending Washington's policies. The presi-

◄ Thomas Jefferson was in favor of states' rights.

dent and vice president were Federalists—people who supported a strong national government. Opposing them were politicians led by future president Thomas Jefferson. These people, called Republicans, thought a strong national government would weaken the power of state governments and limit the rights of citizens. The Federalists and Republicans (also called Democratic-Republicans) became the first two political parties in the United States.

For most of Adams's adult life, his parents had urged him to serve his country somehow. Yet Adams had decided that he liked his life as it was. Still, when President Washington asked him to become the U.S. **minister** to the Netherlands, Adams could not refuse. He arrived in the Netherlands in October 1794. His father was elected president two years later.

The Netherlands ▼ around the time that Adams was appointed minister to that country

For the next seven years, Adams held various posts in Europe. During his stay in Europe, Adams sometimes traveled to London, England. On a trip there in 1795, he began to visit Louisa Johnson. Louisa was the daughter of an American official in London. Like Adams, she was intelligent and spoke perfect French. Also like him, she had a strong personality. They married in 1797.

▼ *Louisa Johnson Adams*

Although they loved each other, the two often disagreed. Adams sometimes had trouble dealing with a woman who would not back down. During their long marriage, they had three sons. They also had a daughter, who died as a child.

Serving at Home and Abroad

★ ★ ★

In 1801, John Quincy Adams returned to Boston and his law practice. He struggled to find clients. For a time, he thought about quitting law and moving west. In his heart, Adams would have preferred to have been a writer or a scientist.

By 1802, however, Adams gave up on moving and decided to enter politics. Running as a Federalist, Adams was elected to the Massachusetts state senate. The following March, the state leaders chose him to represent Massachusetts in the U.S. Senate.

Adams was not popular in Washington, D.C. Many senators had not liked President Adams. Their dislike carried over to his son. Some people also thought the younger Adams was hard to get along with. Even other Federalists did not always like him because he did not follow the party's positions.

Adams became involved in Massachusetts politics and met with other leaders in the Old State House in Boston.

The ceremony of land ▲ transfer from France to the United States that sealed the Louisiana Purchase in 1804

Adams believed in doing what he thought was best for the country, even if others did not agree. Adams voted for the Louisiana Purchase of 1803. In this deal, France sold the United States a huge stretch of land between the Mississippi River and the Rocky Mountains. It doubled the size of the country. Most Federalists opposed the purchase. They thought the northeastern states would lose political power if the country expanded. Adams, however, believed the purchase would make the entire country stronger in the end.

The conflict between Adams and the Federalists grew worse in 1807. At the time, British warships sometimes stopped U.S. merchant ships. They were looking for British sailors who had fled the navy. In June, the

▼ *An American merchant ship at port in Philadelphia*

British fired on a U.S. warship because they thought some British sailors were on board. This event angered many Republicans. Most Federalists, however, did not want any trouble with Great Britain.

Adams thought the Republicans were right to be angry. He supported their response. This included an **embargo,** a law that made it illegal to bring foreign goods into the United States. The embargo was meant to hurt the British because they sold many items to U.S. merchants—especially in the Northeast.

British officials ▶ recapturing sailors who had deserted the British navy

Federalists in Mass-
achusetts accused Adams
of being disloyal to the
party. One Federalist said
Adams should "have [his]
head taken off" for sup-
porting the Republicans.

The next year,
Adams lost his seat in the
U.S. Senate. From then
on, he was more of a
Democratic-Republican
than a Federalist.

Adams was not out

▲ *James Madison*

of a job for long. In 1809, he left for Russia. The new president, James Madison, had asked him to serve as U.S. minister there. Adams held that job for almost five years. He
became friends with the Russian leader Alexander I. The
two men took long walks together, speaking in French
about world events.

In 1812, France invaded Russia, and Adams sent
Madison reports on the fighting. The same year, the War of
1812 (1812–1814) broke out between Great Britain and

A battle aboard ship ▶ during the War of 1812

James Monroe, the ▼ president who named Adams secretary of state

the United States. In 1814, Adams traveled to Ghent, Belgium, to help write a peace **treaty,** or agreement, to end the War of 1812. The treaty let the United States keep all the lands it had claimed before the war.

After that, Adams served as the U.S. minister to Great Britain—a job his father had once held. Then, in 1817, the new president, James Monroe, named him secretary of state, his chief adviser on foreign affairs.

Back in the United States, Adams saw how the country had changed since he had left for Europe in 1809. America had entered the so-called Era of Good Feeling. The Federalist Party had started to fade away after the War of 1812. People seemed united behind Monroe and the Democratic-Republicans, and the economy was growing.

As secretary of state, Adams believed the United States had to assert itself in North America. At the time, Spain still controlled part of the West, the Southwest, and eastern Florida. In the Northwest, Great Britain claimed Oregon and surrounding lands. Adams wanted to extend the boundaries of the United States, but he wanted to do it peacefully.

▼ *A trading post in Oregon Territory*

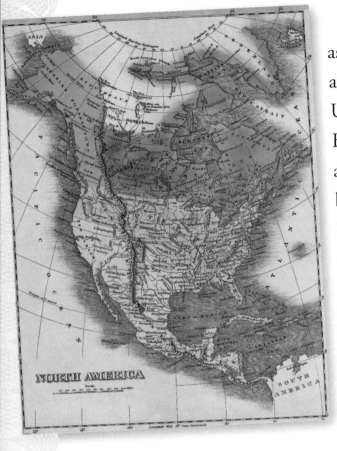

As secretary of state, ▲
Adams was effective at
setting boundaries and
expanding U.S. land.

NORTH AMERICA

Adams's first big success as secretary of state was an agreement between the United States and Great Britain. The two nations agreed on the boundary between Canada and the United States in the West. Great Britain also agreed to allow U.S. citizens to settle freely in Oregon. Soon, Adams had also worked out an agreement in which Spain sold the United States all of Florida.

As secretary of state, Adams was also deeply involved with events outside of the United States. In South and Central America, Spanish colonies had been fighting for independence. By 1822, Mexico, Chile, Colombia, and other areas had become independent. Adams and President Monroe hoped the United States would win the friendship of these countries—and perhaps help shape their affairs.

Many European nations did not like that these colonies had broken away from Spain. France, Russia, and Austria planned to help Spain take back its former colonies. Great Britain wanted the United States to join it in a statement warning these nations against any attack in Central and South America.

Yet Adams did not trust Great Britain. He convinced President Monroe that the United States should make its own statement to the Europeans. Speaking to Congress in December 1823, Monroe outlined the U.S. position to all the European nations—including Great Britain. The United States would not allow any country to set up new colonies in North and South America. Also, the United States would not accept Europeans trying to influence events in independent nations in the Americas. Such

▼ *George IV was king of Great Britain when conflict arose between Spain and its colonies in America.*

efforts, Monroe said, would be "dangerous to our peace and security." In return, the United States would stay out of European wars. The United States would also stay out of the Europeans' colonial affairs in Central and South America.

The new American policy was called the Monroe **Doctrine**, but it was Adams who had shaped it. The Monroe Doctrine was an important step forward for the United States. It showed Europe that the United States was willing to play a larger role in the world, especially in its own region.

A famous painting ▼ by Clyde O. DeLand depicting Monroe (standing) discussing his doctrine with U.S. officials, including John Quincy Adams (seated far left)

A Difficult Four Years

★　★　★

By 1824, the Era of Good Feeling had faded, and the Democratic-Republicans began to split apart. Adams was one of many leaders who decided to run for president that year.

Adams seemed to have an advantage. Secretary of state was one of the nation's most powerful jobs. Three of the first five U.S. presidents had held that job before going to the White House. Adams believed that his years of service made him an ideal **candidate** for president.

Adams faced some problems winning the presidency. Many people still connected him with his father, who had been an unpopular president. The younger Adams was not well liked either. Adams also seemed uncomfortable speaking in front of crowds and asking people for their votes.

Secretary of the ▲
Treasury William
Crawford was popular
with Congress.

Three other men were in the race for president. One was Secretary of the Treasury William Crawford of Georgia. He was popular with Congress. Henry Clay of Kentucky was the Speaker of the House of Representatives. He was well known across the country. Clay supported what he called the American System. He wanted the government to charge a tariff on foreign-made goods. Clay also believed the government should spend money building roads and canals across the country.

The most popular candidate in 1824 was Andrew Jackson of Tennessee. "Old Hickory," as he was called, was a former general and war hero. He had won the last

★

battle of the War of 1812, and in 1818 he had taken control of Spanish forts in Florida.

The election was very close. Jackson won the popular vote. He also won ninety-nine electoral votes to Adams's eighty-four. Clay and Crawford had also won some electoral votes, so no man had more than half. Under the Constitution, when no candidate has more than 50 percent of the electoral votes, the House of Representatives chooses the president.

▼ *Andrew Jackson's famous military victories during the War of 1812 (below) and against Spanish troops in Florida made him a popular presidential candidate in 1824.*

The vote in the House was among Jackson, Adams, and Crawford. Clay had received the fewest electoral votes, so he was out of the running. Yet Clay had a lot of influence in the House. Like Clay, Adams believed the government should play a major role in improving the U.S. economy. Clay also disliked Jackson, so he gave Adams his support.

Henry Clay received too few electoral votes to stay in the race. ◄

Before the House vote, a newspaper reported that Clay and Adams had made a secret deal. Clay would help Adams win if Adams named him secretary of state. Both men denied the claim, but Jackson did not believe them. Jackson wrote that Clay and Adams had made a "corrupt bargain" that kept him from becoming president.

Adams won the vote in the House of Representatives. The close election and the rumors of a secret deal, however, would create problems for the new president.

As president, Adams went forward with Clay's American System. He supported the tariff. This would help promote American goods by making foreign goods more expensive. Adams also wanted to build roads and canals. These would make it easier for Americans to settle lands in the West and for merchants to transport their goods there.

Adams's plans, however, were not popular in Congress. Some people thought Adams was trying to

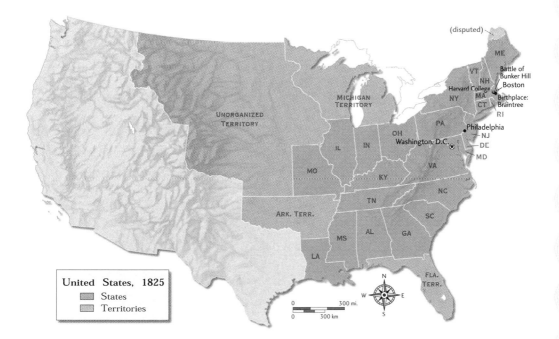

United States, 1825
States
Territories

President John ▲ Quincy Adams

claim too much power for the national government. They thought it would hurt the power of the states. Jackson was already planning to run again for president. He began to call himself a supporter of the "common man." He said Adams favored the wealthy and powerful.

By 1826, Congress was controlled by people who opposed Adams. They refused to give him as much money as he asked for new programs. He also didn't have their support in his dealings with other countries. Adams struggled with the many problems he faced. In 1827, he wrote, "The weight grows heavier from day to day."

Despite the difficulties of his job, Adams followed daily routines that helped relax him. He awoke each day between 5 and 6 A.M. and usually took a long walk by himself through Washington. It was just a small town then. Presidents did not travel with large security forces, as they do now.

After his morning exercise, Adams read his Bible. Then he began his daily events. These usually included meeting guests, reading papers, and writing in his diary.

▲ *A view of Washington, D.C., at around the time Adams was president*

During the summers, Adams and his family briefly escaped the hot, humid capital and visited their farm in Quincy, Massachusetts. The trip Adams made there in 1826 was the saddest, as he returned home to visit his dying father. Before reaching Massachusetts, Adams learned that his father had died on July 4, the fiftieth anniversary of the adoption of the Declaration of Independence. John Adams had fought hard for independence. He and John Quincy were the first American father and son to serve their country as president. In his diary, President John Quincy Adams wrote that his father "served to great and useful purpose his nation, his age, and his God."

The Adams's family farm in Quincy ▶

Martin Van Buren ▼

As Adams did his best to work with Congress, his political enemies planned for the 1828 election. In Congress, Senator Martin Van Buren of New York was a strong supporter of Andrew Jackson. Van Buren worked to unite Northerners and Southerners who opposed

★

Adams. His efforts led to the birth of the Democratic Party. In general, the Democrats supported a limited national government. They also supported the spread of slavery into new U.S. territories.

When election time came, Old Hickory's Democratic supporters organized barbecues, parades, and other events to support Jackson. The National Republicans, Adams's party, did the same for the president. Both sides used the newspapers to spread lies about the other.

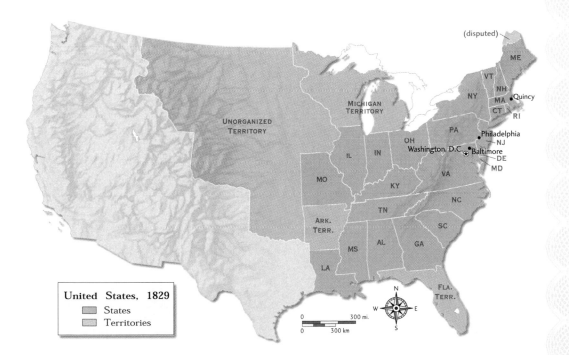

United States, 1829
- States
- Territories

Adams was never popular with most Americans. He did not stand a chance against the war hero Jackson. Adams won eighty-three electoral votes, all coming from the Northeast. Jackson, meanwhile, won twice as many electoral votes and earned 56 percent of the popular votes.

Jackson won the ▼ presidency in 1828.

"Old Man Eloquent" Attacks Slavery

★   ★   ★

After losing the election, Adams wrote, studied, and kept track of President Jackson and his actions. In September 1830, a friend in Massachusetts suggested he run for the House of Representatives. Adams said he felt too old and sick to run, but he said he would serve if the people voted for him. He easily won the election. He was the first former president to serve in Congress.

One of Adams's first acts in the House was to introduce

◄ President Andrew Jackson

As a congressman, Adams worked to end the slave trade.

several petitions about slavery. A petition is a request by voters that the government consider an issue. The petitions Adams brought to the House called for the end of the slave trade and slavery in Washington, D.C. Although Adams personally opposed slavery, he thought discussing it in the House would "lead to ill will, to heart burnings, to mutual hatred." Still, he thought American citizens had a right to have their petitions heard by Congress.

Slavery was already an emotional issue in the United States. Some people, mostly in the North, wanted to end slavery at once. Others simply wanted to keep it from spreading into new territories and states that entered the Union. In the South, slavery was an important part of the economy. Most Southerners did not want any limits on slavery. They believed the voters in each state had the right to decide if slavery should be allowed. Some people,

◄ *One of many heated debates in Congress over the issue of slavery*

Members of ▲ the House of Representatives debate the gag rule in 1836

including Adams, thought that slavery might one day divide the nation in two.

In 1836, supporters of President Jackson passed a rule in the House. They declared that the House would not read or consider any petition on slavery. This **"gag rule"** took away the right of U.S. citizens to express their opinions on slavery through their representatives. Adams knew slavery was an explosive issue. Still, he thought citizens should be able to bring up any topic with their government.

Over the next eight years, as Adams entered his seventies, he led the attack on the gag rule. He read petitions that did not use the word slavery, even though they clearly were about it. He also spoke out against the gag rule. His speeches, on this and other issues, earned him the nickname "Old Man **Eloquent**." The speeches against the gag rule also won him enemies. At one point, his enemies tried to have him thrown out of Congress.

Adams believed the Declaration of Independence and the Constitution gave everyone, including slaves, legal rights. Yet that belief did not mean he wanted to end slavery at once. Adams thought that the South would form its own country before it ever let the U.S. government end slavery. Adams wanted to keep the country together. Still, he used every opportunity he could to question slavery.

▼ *John Quincy Adams during his later years*

Jospeh Cinque, leader of the 1841 revolt aboard the Amistad

In 1841, Adams tried to win the freedom of fifty-three Africans. The Africans had been captured by Spanish slave traders and taken to Cuba, an island in the Caribbean. They then sailed from one Cuban port to another on the ship *Amistad.* The Africans attacked their captors and took control of the ship. The captives ended up off the shore of New York. There, they were thrown in jail. They waited almost two years to learn if they were slaves or free people.

Martin Van Buren, now the U.S. president, argued that the Africans should be turned over to Spain. Adams believed the slave traders had broken the law in taking the Africans in the first place. The case finally reached the U.S.

Supreme Court. Adams defended the Africans before the
Court. He referred to the Declaration of Independence,
saying, "the moment you come to . . . [the part] that every
man has a right to life and liberty, this case is decided." The

▼ *Adams used the
Declaration of
Independence in his
defense of the
African prisoners.*

Supreme Court
agreed and ordered
that the Africans
be released.

Adams won his
last major political
victory in 1844.
He finally con-
vinced enough
representatives to
vote for ending
the gag rule. After
the vote, Adams
wrote in his diary,
"Blessed, forever
blessed, be the
name of God!"

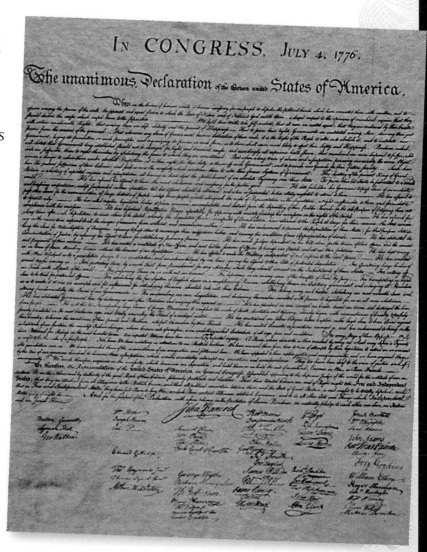

A Fitting End

★ ★ ★

During his last few years in Congress, Adams grew weak with old age. Yet his beliefs stayed strong. He opposed letting Texas enter the Union because slavery was legal there. In 1846, Adams was one of just eleven House members who voted against going to war with Mexico. The war, Adams believed, was an excuse to take control of new lands and bring slavery to them.

On February 21, 1848, Adams showed his lasting dislike for the Mexican War. He voted against a proposal to honor U.S. veterans of the war. Then, standing to speak, he began to fall. He had suffered a **stroke.** Another representative caught him before he hit the floor. Adams died two days later.

Adams sometimes felt he had not done enough with his life. He thought he could have been a better person. His presidency was not a successful one. Adams won

◄ *Adams collapsed in Congress on February 21, 1848.*

praise, however, for his service as secretary of state and for his brave actions in the House of Representatives. During his long life, John Quincy Adams always used his intelligence and strong faith to serve his country and support liberty.

The tombs of John Quincy Adams and Louisa Adams in Quincy, Massachusetts

GLOSSARY

★ ★ ★

candidate—someone running for office in an election

colonies—territories settled by people from another country and ruled by that country

diplomat—person who represents his or her government in a foreign country

doctrine—a basic principle

eloquent—able to speak in a powerful and convincing way

embargo—a law that outlaws bringing certain foreign goods into a country

fencing—the art of using swords

gag rule—a rule against talking about something

minister—an official who represents one's country in another country

secretary of state—a president's top adviser on foreign affairs

stroke—a problem in the brain causing a sudden loss of the ability to feel or move

tariff—a tax placed on certain foreign goods entering a country

translator—someone who changes one language into another

treaty—an agreement between two governments

JOHN QUINCY ADAMS'S LIFE AT A GLANCE

★ ★ ★

PERSONAL

Nickname:	"Old Man Eloquent"
Birth date:	July 11, 1767
Birthplace:	Braintree (Quincy), Massachusetts
Father's name:	John Adams
Mother's name:	Abigail Adams
Education:	Graduated from Harvard College in 1787
Wife's name:	Louisa Catherine Johnson Adams (1775–1852)
Married:	July 26, 1797
Children:	George Washington Adams (1801–1829); John Adams (1803–1834); Charles Francis Adams (1807–1886); Louisa Catherine Adams (1811–1812)
Died:	February 23, 1848, in Washington, D.C.
Buried:	First Unitarian Church in Quincy, Massachusetts

PUBLIC

Occupation before presidency:	Lawyer, writer
Occupation after presidency:	Representative from Massachusetts in the U.S. House of Representatives; lawyer
Military service:	None
Other government positions:	Member of the Massachusetts Senate; U.S. senator from Massachusetts; U.S. minister to Russia; U.S. minister to Great Britain; secretary of state
Political party:	Democratic-Republican
Vice president:	John C. Calhoun
Dates in office:	March 4, 1825–March 4, 1829
Presidential opponents:	Henry Clay (Democratic-Republican), William H. Crawford (Democratic-Republican), Andrew Jackson (Democratic-Republican), 1824; Andrew Jackson (Democrat), 1828
Number of votes (Electoral College):	108,740 of 356,740 (84 of 261), 1824; 508,064 of 1,155,350 (83 of 261), 1828
Selected Writings:	*Writings of John Quincy Adams* (7 vols., 1913–1917)

John Quincy Adams's Cabinet

Secretary of state:
  Henry Clay (1825–1829)

Secretary of the treasury:
  Richard Rush (1825–1829)

Secretary of war:
  James Barbour (1825–1828)
  Peter B. Porter (1828)

Attorney general:
  William Wirt (1825–1829)

Secretary of the navy:
  Samuel L. Southard (1825–1829)

JOHN QUINCY ADAMS'S LIFE AND TIMES

★ ★ ★

ADAMS'S LIFE		WORLD EVENTS	
July 11, Adams is born in Braintree, Massachusetts	1767		
		1769	British explorer Captain James Cook reaches New Zealand
	1770	1770	Five die in a street clash that becomes known as the Boston Massacre (below)
Travels to Europe with his father	1777	1777	Vermont is the first former colony to ban slavery
		1779	Jan Ingenhousz of the Netherlands discovers that plants release oxygen when exposed to sunlight

ADAMS'S LIFE

WORLD EVENTS

1780

Serves as a translator
for a U.S. diplomat
in Russia — 1781

1783 American author
Washington Irving is
born

1786 Frontiersman Davy
Crockett is born in
Greene County,
Tennessee

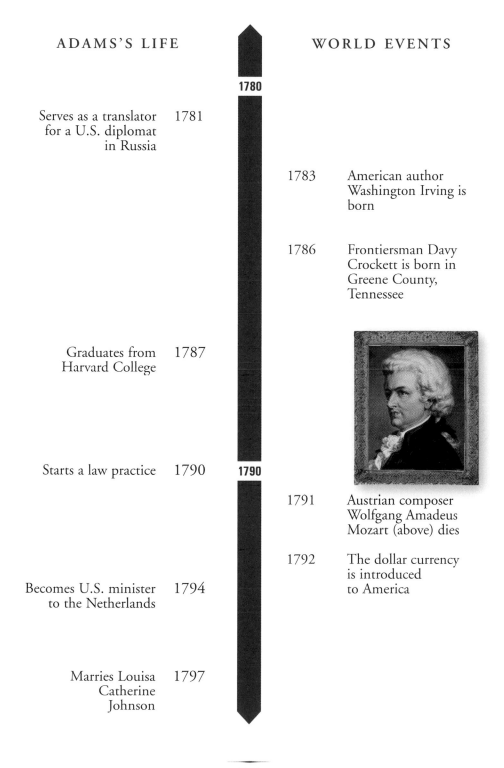

Graduates from 1787
Harvard College

Starts a law practice 1790 **1790**

1791 Austrian composer
Wolfgang Amadeus
Mozart (above) dies

1792 The dollar currency
is introduced
to America

Becomes U.S. minister 1794
to the Netherlands

Marries Louisa 1797
Catherine
Johnson

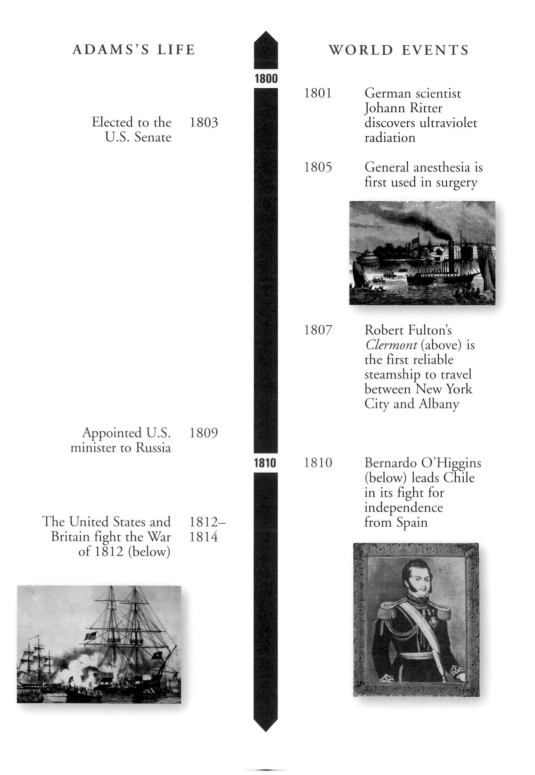

ADAMS'S LIFE

Elected to the   1803
U.S. Senate

Appointed U.S.   1809
minister to Russia

The United States and   1812–
Britain fight the War   1814
of 1812 (below)

1800

1810

WORLD EVENTS

1801   German scientist
        Johann Ritter
        discovers ultraviolet
        radiation

1805   General anesthesia is
        first used in surgery

1807   Robert Fulton's
        Clermont (above) is
        the first reliable
        steamship to travel
        between New York
        City and Albany

1810   Bernardo O'Higgins
        (below) leads Chile
        in its fight for
        independence
        from Spain

ADAMS'S LIFE		WORLD EVENTS	
Becomes U.S. minister to England	1815	1814–1815	European states meet in Vienna to redraw national borders after the Napoleonic Wars
Appointed secretary of state	1817	1817	New York begins construction of the Erie Canal, which will link the Great Lakes to the Atlantic Ocean
	1820	1820	Susan B. Anthony (below), a leader of the American woman suffrage movement, is born
President James Monroe (above) proclaims the Monroe Doctrine, which Adams helped develop	1823		

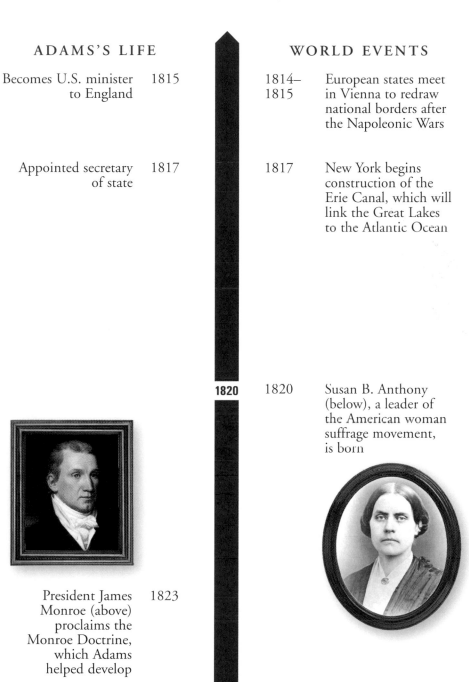

ADAMS'S LIFE

1824 None of the four candidates for president wins a majority of the electoral votes; the election is thrown into the House of Representatives, whose members vote for Adams

Presidential Election Results:	Popular Votes	Electoral Votes
1824 John Q. Adams	108,740	84
Andrew Jackson	153,544	99
Henry Clay	47,136	37
William H. Crawford	46,618	41

1825 After the election controversy, the Democratic-Republican Party splits into the National Republicans, who supported Adams, and the Democratic-Republicans, who supported Andrew Jackson

1828 Adams loses to Andrew Jackson in his bid for a second term

WORLD EVENTS

1824 The U.S. Army sets up outposts in present-day Oklahoma in preparation for the removal of the Cherokee and Choctaw tribes from the southeastern United States

1826 The world's first photograph is taken by French physicist Joseph Niépce

1829 The first practical sewing machine is invented by French tailor Barthélemy Thimonnier (above)

ADAMS'S LIFE

WORLD EVENTS

Elected to the U.S. House of Representatives — 1830

1830

1833 — Great Britain abolishes slavery

1836 — Texans defeat Mexican troops at San Jacinto after a deadly battle at the Alamo

1840 — 1840 — Auguste Rodin, famous sculptor of *The Thinker* (below), is born in France

In an argument before the Supreme Court, wins the freedom of the slaves who took over the *Amistad* — 1841

Gains enough support to overturn the gag rule on slavery petitions — 1844

February 21, suffers a stroke in the House of Representatives; dies two days later — 1848

1848 — *The Communist Manifesto,* by German writer Karl Marx, is widely distributed

UNDERSTANDING JOHN QUINCY ADAMS AND HIS PRESIDENCY

★ ★ ★

IN THE LIBRARY

Collier, Christopher. *Andrew Jackson's America, 1824–1850.*
New York: Benchmark Books, 1999.

Freedman, Suzanne. *United States v. Amistad: Rebellion on a Slave Ship.*
Berkeley Heights, N.J.: Enslow Publishers, 2000.

Harness, Cheryl. *Young John Quincy.*
New York: Bradbury Press, 1994.

Joseph, Paul. *John Quincy Adams.*
Edina, Minn.: Abdo Publishing Company, 1999.

ON THE WEB

Adams Papers
www.masshist.org/adams.html
For the important writings of many members of the
Adams family, including John, Abigail, and John Quincy

The American President—John Quincy Adams
www.americanpresident.org/KoTRain/Courses/JADM/JADM_In_Brief.htm
For basic facts about Adams and his times,
as well as quotes and links to other sources

Internet Public Library—John Quincy Adams
www.ipl.org/ref/POTUS/JADMdams.html
For information about John Quincy Adams's life and presidency

ADAMS HISTORIC SITES
ACROSS THE COUNTRY

Adams National Historical Park
1250 Hancock Street
Quincy, MA 02169
617/770-1175
To see the home where John Quincy Adams
was born and where he lived as an adult

Mystic Seaport
Amistad Exhibit
75 Greenmanville Avenue
P.O. Box 6000
Mystic, CT 06355-0990
888/973-2767
To see a replica of the *Amistad*
and learn more about the case

United First Parish Church
1306 Hancock Street (Quincy Center)
Quincy, MA 02169
617/773-1290
To visit Adams's grave site

THE U.S. PRESIDENTS
(Years in Office)

★ ★ ★

1. **George Washington**
   (March 4, 1789-March 3, 1797)
2. **John Adams**
   (March 4, 1797-March 3, 1801)
3. **Thomas Jefferson**
   (March 4, 1801-March 3, 1809)
4. **James Madison**
   (March 4, 1809-March 3, 1817)
5. **James Monroe**
   (March 4, 1817-March 3, 1825)
6. **John Quincy Adams**
   (March 4, 1825-March 3, 1829)
7. **Andrew Jackson**
   (March 4, 1829-March 3, 1837)
8. **Martin Van Buren**
   (March 4, 1837-March 3, 1841)
9. **William Henry Harrison**
   (March 6, 1841-April 4, 1841)
10. **John Tyler**
    (April 6, 1841-March 3, 1845)
11. **James K. Polk**
    (March 4, 1845-March 3, 1849)
12. **Zachary Taylor**
    (March 5, 1849-July 9, 1850)
13. **Millard Fillmore**
    (July 10, 1850-March 3, 1853)
14. **Franklin Pierce**
    (March 4, 1853-March 3, 1857)
15. **James Buchanan**
    (March 4, 1857-March 3, 1861)
16. **Abraham Lincoln**
    (March 4, 1861-April 15, 1865)
17. **Andrew Johnson**
    (April 15, 1865-March 3, 1869)

18. **Ulysses S. Grant**
    (March 4, 1869-March 3, 1877)
19. **Rutherford B. Hayes**
    (March 4, 1877-March 3, 1881)
20. **James Garfield**
    (March 4, 1881-Sept 19, 1881)
21. **Chester Arthur**
    (Sept 20, 1881-March 3, 1885)
22. **Grover Cleveland**
    (March 4, 1885-March 3, 1889)
23. **Benjamin Harrison**
    (March 4, 1889-March 3, 1893)
24. **Grover Cleveland**
    (March 4, 1893-March 3, 1897)
25. **William McKinley**
    (March 4, 1897-
    September 14, 1901)
26. **Theodore Roosevelt**
    (September 14, 1901-
    March 3, 1909)
27. **William Howard Taft**
    (March 4, 1909-March 3, 1913)
28. **Woodrow Wilson**
    (March 4, 1913-March 3, 1921)
29. **Warren G. Harding**
    (March 4, 1921-August 2, 1923)
30. **Calvin Coolidge**
    (August 3, 1923-March 3, 1929)
31. **Herbert Hoover**
    (March 4, 1929-March 3, 1933)
32. **Franklin D. Roosevelt**
    (March 4, 1933-April 12, 1945)

33. **Harry S. Truman**
    (April 12, 1945-
    January 20, 1953)
34. **Dwight D. Eisenhower**
    (January 20, 1953-
    January 20, 1961)
35. **John F. Kennedy**
    (January 20, 1961-
    November 22, 1963)
36. **Lyndon B. Johnson**
    (November 22, 1963-
    January 20, 1969)
37. **Richard M. Nixon**
    (January 20, 1969-
    August 9, 1974)
38. **Gerald R. Ford**
    (August 9, 1974-
    January 20, 1977)
39. **James Earl Carter**
    (January 20, 1977-
    January 20, 1981)
40. **Ronald Reagan**
    (January 20, 1981-
    January 20, 1989)
41. **George H. W. Bush**
    (January 20, 1989-
    January 20, 1993)
42. **William Jefferson Clinton**
    (January 20, 1993-
    January 20, 2001)
43. **George W. Bush**
    (January 20, 2001-)

INDEX

★ ★ ★

ABOUT THE AUTHOR
Michael Burgan is a freelance writer of books for children and adults. A history graduate of the University of Connecticut, he has written more than thirty fiction and nonfiction children's books for various publishers. For adult audiences, he has written news articles, essays, and plays. Michael Burgan is a recipient of an Edpress Award and belongs to the Society of Children's Book Writers and Illustrators.

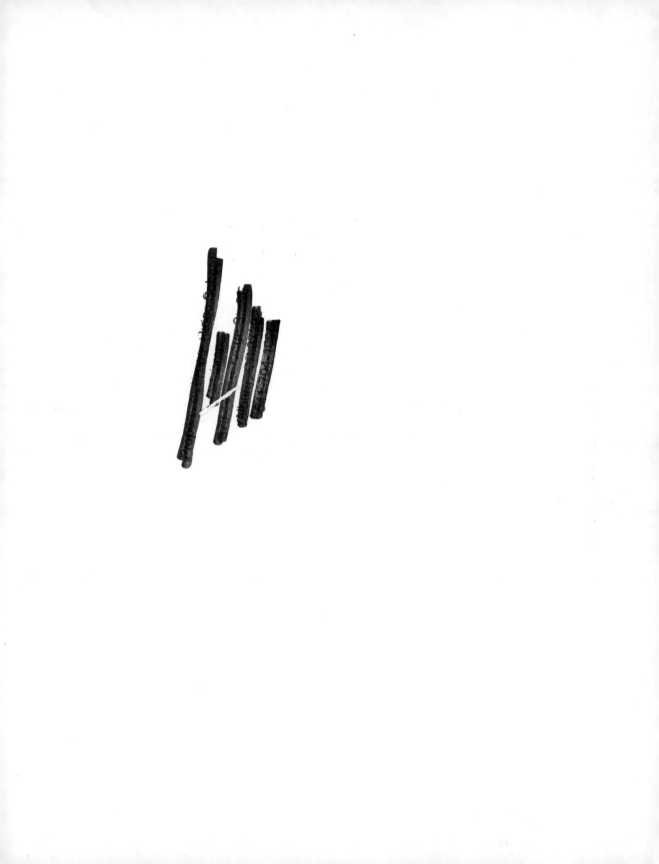